all my favorite men

are dead

a healing book of pain

all my favorite men are dead

copyright © 2022 by női lélek

ISBN 979-8-9864917-0-7

Editor: Shelby Leigh
Designer: Chris Reale

First Edition

for Monica

i wouldn't be here today if not for you
thank you for witnessing all of my pain
thank you for loving me through it

coming soon from női lélek

also, men are garbage
a healing book of questioning

hu(men)
a healing book of rediscovery

---

fear is the thing with tethers
a recollection of childhood

scan the QR code above for info about
yoga+poetry trauma healing workshops

this collection comes with
the following content warnings:

- sexual assault
- rape
- pedophilia
- mental health conditions
- self-harm
- suicidal ideation
- disassociation
- PTSD

please be safe. take breaks as needed.
your mental & emotional health are most important.
always.

introduction

every other page of this book is empty so that you
– the reader – can fill it with YOUR truth.

write, draw, sketch, paint, journal, collage…
use these pages to create anything that feels true to you.
do whatever feels right – whatever will best
help you work through YOUR pain, YOUR trauma, and all of the
big and small ways in which this world has also broken YOU.

you are not alone.
in your anger. in your fear.
in your overwhelming sadness.
in your desperation to feel safe again.
you are not alone.

i hope you do write on every single page
(even the ones i haven't left blank).
i don't want this to be just a book of my poetry,
but a co-creation between the two of us.
two women, completely unknown to each other,
sharing the worst that life has done to them and given to them,
and in so doing, lessening both our suffering.

i don't know you, but i know that
you have done nothing to deserve what's happened to you.
and i know that
you are worthy of all the love and kindness in the world.
and my greatest hope is that, by releasing your pain
on the pages of this book, you're able to see that as clearly as i do.
for it is the truest truth i have ever known.

- all my favorite men are dead -

i feel like if a guy found a hole in my heart,
he'd want to stick his dick in that too

in the center of the garden

i'll share with you
the parts of me
no one ever gets to see
so that you can also know
so that it too can weigh heavy on your soul
and eat away at any joy
you managed to save throughout the day
in the quiet spaces of your mind
before you fall asleep at night
only to wake
once more
to the same cruel fate:

knowing

- all my favorite men are dead -

violated

i hate this body
i'm forced to live in
i know it wants me dead
it tells me all the time
i hear its whispers in my head

i hate this mind
i can't escape
every thought is like a knife
carving away
at the ropes that bind me
to my own discarded life

i hate this heart that beats
so haphazardly in my chest
doesn't it know its days are numbered
doesn't it realize i couldn't care less

if i have a soul
i hate that too
if for no other reason
than it's also a part of me –
just one more thing
for broken men to screw

if there is a maker to be met
one day when i'm free
i'll spit in his fucking face
and treat him no better
than this world has treated me

i like it
like that

if by that
you mean
i don't like it
at all
i never have

- all my favorite men are dead -

crazy bitch

i don't have to act crazy
I am.

my mind has been stolen
by the men who never treated me
as if i had one of my own

the girl i couldn't save

I am haunted
by the girl i couldn't save
the one whose name
still lingers on my lips
a reminder of
who i was
when he did
what he did

her figure lives
in my memory
broken and spent
because she can't pass on
i can never forget

her pain
her fear
the silence of
her tears

the ghosts
i grow to know
more intimately
with each passing year

the moon stayed in the sky
an entire lifetime that night
and by morning
she was dead

a loss
only i observed
a failure
i alone regret

- all my favorite men are dead -

this body
is the coffin
i lie in
while alive

it looks perfect
or so i've been told
by men i barely know

but what it's best at
is keeping Me
trapped quietly inside

i stare at the coals
i imagine i stoked
a lifetime ago
when i first felt cold

- all my favorite men are dead -

preyed upon

and without warning
the hunt was on...
a friendly foe/false friend
leapt from under cover
of my trust
i made no decision
but surrendered my spirit
and lost
more than he won

how do you not understand?

most don't do it because they hate us

they do it because they can

- all my favorite men are dead -

- all my favorite men are dead -

the night that never happened

on the night that never happened
i made it home
alone

on the night that never happened
i never once doubted
the boy i'd always known

on the night that never happened
there were no screams inside my head
no tears down my cheeks
no bruises on my legs

on the night that never happened
i slept – drunkenly, yet peacefully
in my own bed

on the night that never happened
i jokingly swore i'd never drink again

and on the morning after
the night that never happened
i laughed at the memory
of the things i had done and said
and hoped that i would have more nights
like the night that never happened

nights that wouldn't haunt me
wouldn't change me irrevocably

nights i could simply enjoy,
and then forget

the eyes i fear

i walk alone
looking for peace
the chance to breathe
forgetting, again
I am a woman

their stares intrude
upon my solitude
they watch me as i pass by

and it scares me

i can see myself in their eyes
the image of it –
me –
haunts my thoughts
both awake and asleep

because what they see
isn't even a human being

my body
reflected in their eyes
is just another
unlikely possibility
a challenge to be accepted
a war to be fought
one more shot
at a perverse victory

their fantasies –
my nightmares –
are written across their faces
like words on a page
of a book i hope to never read

for if i ever did…
if i were to look at me
and only see what they see

i fear
it would be
the very end
of my humanity

of Me

- all my favorite men are dead -

they say
do not fear men
you paranoid woman
you crazy bitch
you angry feminist cunt
in need of a dick

but then,
when it happens
the worst thing of all

they say
you should have seen this coming
you should have known this would happen
stupid slut
you deserve what you got

so excuse me,
if i no longer care
what *they* say

for i've finally realized
the plan was always to damn me
either way

can i continue to be

i like it better
when no one is here
the voice whispered
to no one around

and i had to agree
i also prefer
when it's just me
and no one can i
continue to be

- all my favorite men are dead -

- all my favorite men are dead -

men will never understand
you can't pretend
you can only hope
to never have to
go through it
again

a voice
so solid, so steady
came to me once in a dream
it said it wanted to protect me
but why then did it scream?

- all my favorite men are dead -

take back the night

is there more
to life
than dead neon
on a soulless night

ask not the men
who prowl these streets
and see only flesh
only choice
pieces of meat

evidence

the scratches
tell a story:
where i've been
but also,
what i did
and what was done
to me –
with and without
my consent

- all my favorite men are dead -

- all my favorite men are dead -

I am a woman

i cannot be alone
i cannot simply exist

I am a woman

it just isn't my lot in life
though it is my deepest wish

to every complete and total stranger
who couldn't take a hint:

STOP STARING AT ME

DON'T FUCKING TALK TO ME

LEAVE. ME. ALONE.

- all my favorite men are dead -

- all my favorite men are dead -

who I am today

i can be
no one else

this world created me
and therefore,
is stuck with
the me
it has created

the me
it continues to
create

out of fear
out of hate

girl, chick, slut, cunt, heifer, thot, bitch

a woman
by any other name
would be as disregarded
and yet,
equally as much a target
to those with the power
to point and lay claim

- all my favorite men are dead -

- all my favorite men are dead -

the hell women live

terror
is the shame
of having been afraid
but also, the anger
that comes with knowing
had anything happened
you would have been to blame

all fun and games until...

i thought they'd kill me
when they were done
but they just walked away
smiling, high-fiving
winners all
my body, their game

- *all my favorite men are dead* -

and now even the most tender caress
incites the phantom pain again
of his hand on my neck
and the thrust of a knife
into my broken
f l   Es.   h

i don't know what's safe

i don't know what's safe
and what's dangerous
i cut myself until i bleed
but run away
from anyone who claims to care about me
i get comfort
imagining all the ways i'll die
i feel reckless
lying next to the man i love
and just closing my eyes
i think something broke in my mind –
ten years ago almost to the day –
i assumed the best
right before the worst
and you see,
i've never really been the same

- all my favorite men are dead -

invisible bars

i'm shackled to a life
i refuse to believe exists
i wake each morning
begging for release
wondering when
if
i'll ever be free

captive

i've been talked at
by men
i'd only just met

lost hundreds of hours
i'll never get back

prey in a trap
society sets
to hold us all captive
with compliments and threats

- all my favorite men are dead -

- all my favorite men are dead -

monsters

we talk of vampires
and you think it's silly i'm afraid
but i know monsters exist
for i learned my lesson long ago
and the body
i used to think of as my own
wasn't the only price i paid

why do women understand
what no man can
why do i feel safe
around all other women
and not even a single man

- all my favorite men are dead -

- all my favorite men are dead -

never will i ever
walk without fear
of all that could happen
should the wrong man appear

never will i ever
know how it feels
to be seen as impenetrable
as if made of steel

never will i ever
live in a world
where i will be praised
for running
or hitting
or succeeding
like a girl

never will i ever
be number one
for sitting down
and just getting it done

never will i ever
know what it's like
to live at the top
and bask in that light

never will i ever
be anything
but what I am
a woman
a female and –
in the eyes of men –
a second-class
citizen

"you need to be more friendly,"
a man once told me
smiling
right before he sold me

- all my favorite men are dead -

because i have no other choice

right now
in this moment
alone in this old building
I am trusting this man
not to hurt me
to do his job and leave
to not realize
or at least, not take advantage
of the differences in our size
his strength vs mine
I am trusting him
because i have to
because i have no other choice
because society has decided
all men are trustworthy
until proven otherwise
and even then,
should be given another chance
to prove their abilities
to respect our humanity even if
they repeatedly disrespect our bodies
so here I am, sitting on a stair
him, working over there
completely unaware
of how acutely aware I am
that it is i, not he
whose trust is being tested
that it is i, not he
who would bear the scars forever
were anything to happen

the tornado inside
destroyed everything
i once loved;
and though i didn't move
the entire night,
by morning
i was gone

- all my favorite men are dead -

how silly of me

strange men scream at me
for resisting

i'm sorry, how silly of me
for existing

but still he came
though i was not of age
though he knew not my name
though i cried and begged
to be taken away from this world
and this pain
still, still
he came

- all my favorite men are dead -

my life sentence

my memories are a prison
to which i've been sentenced
for life

escape isn't an option
for on the day i'm finally free
i die

whether you like it or not

and you'll be a woman whether you like it or not
so you better like it
for centuries to come
and force your daughters to like it
and theirs
and theirs after
and we shall be raising our sons
to curse and rape, belittle and denigrate
to kill your daughters' spirits
loot their bodies for its treasure
and leave behind their waste
to create more sons – the men of the future –
shining beacons squalling their demands
at your daughters' breasts
suckling out whatever's left
perpetuating the cycle that keeps
half the human race in check

whether you like it or not

so you better like it
you stupid little slut
you don't know how good you've got it
here in *the land of the free*
you don't know how lucky you are

- all my favorite men are dead -

mad woman

the mad woman in my attic
started to scream again
i'd ask her to stop
but i can no longer imagine
a life without her pain

it's like she screams
so i don't have to
so that i can go on
pretending to be sane

i never wanted
to be this woman
to fear
and hate
with everything i have
everything I am

i never wanted
to be so broken
to still not know
how much of my body
is covered
in undiscovered
scars
missing pieces
of my soul
i'll be searching for
the rest of my life
and still
never be whole

i never wanted
to be homeless
in a borrowed body
i keep discarding
trying to get rid of the pain
of just remembering
your name –
your perverse claim
to fame
in the history
of my life

i never wanted
to be the girl
whose past
destroyed all promise
of a future
without
multiple suicide attempts
anything-but-empty
self death threats
a heart begging
for the bliss
of eternal sedation
fully aware
of certain damnation
a festering internal mutilation
of the soul
the heart
the mind
anything i could get my hands on
to stop –
because i couldn't go back in –
time
and undo the first moment

i never wanted
to be alive

- all my favorite men are dead -

- all my favorite men are dead -

excuses, excuses
i drowned
in a sea of excuses
i made for the sailors
who swore
they'd teach me to swim
if only i'd be a good lass
if only i'd lay back
and take what was given

some / body

they used to tell me
winking, smiling
one day i'd grow
into my own body
now they tell me
i don't know what's right
for my own body
soon they'll tell me
i have no rights
to my own body
that's when i'll know for sure
they only ever saw me
as just some
body

- all my favorite men are dead -

- all my favorite men are dead -

screams in silence
oft forgotten
linger here with me
screams in silence
misbegotten
feed into my misery

no one can hear
what never was said
and yet,
sharp and clear
they echo through my head

shadows of a past
pain as bright as light
these screams that only i can hear
haunt my days
with visions of the night

and even as i live
i know
i have died

the patriarchy

there's a man
inside me
i don't know when
he moved in
or worse, who it was
that let him in

he made himself a home
deep inside my body
and likes to remind me
now and again
that he's here to stay
he says he's a friend

but that's what they all say
or so i've been told
these men in our bodies
digging for gold

excavating treasure
in the mines of our hearts
stealing our sanity
just to rip it apart

i want him out
i want him gone
i want what's mine back
where it belongs

but i'm afraid
this demon
not i
will have the final say

after all
what's a woman
to a man
but a flesh and blood
buffet

- all my favorite men are dead -

- all my favorite men are dead -

i can't breathe
with how much you've given to me
everything, but oxygen it seems
to fill my lungs,
my heart,
every single drop
of blood as it travels through
what remains
of the body you've long taken away
to do with
as you please
and what, you ask
when i beg for it back
would anyone want with me?
what could even be done
with such a sickly, pathetic, half-gone, half-not
thing
I am me
or at least i was
until you
now I am 1/10th of a we
one piece of the whole that is
you
you
you
consume and i, i, i,
feed
and i, i
bleed
and i
breed
and
no longer exist

to succeed at life
you must fail at being a woman
to be a woman
you must give up on life
and create anew

a race will be run
but you won't be entered
your place – by choice
or force – is forfeit
and loss,
all you've won

- all my favorite men are dead -

i've never seen my father cry
what has that done to me,
i wonder?

how fucked up
are my heart and mind
because i've never seen
my father cry?

it started when i was 12

i don't like leaving my home
there's always the possibility
i'll be objectified and dehumanized
by a complete and total stranger
just because i'm a woman

i guess that's why i feel more human when i'm alone

- all my favorite men are dead -

- all my favorite men are dead -

so softly monsters sink their claws

so softly monsters sink their claws
into another's flesh
just when all wounds had closed up
surely i knew that final stitch
was too good to be true
for here we are again
and I am forced to live in fear
not of monster's claws
but that my work to heal from these scars
shall never truly end

disassociate

i stepped outside the pain
and walked into an existence
no man could ever name
one where i ceased
to dream
to feel
to be
one where i looked down on me
where i lay in that bed
with nothing more
than bitter apathy

- all my favorite men are dead -

- all my favorite men are dead -

misogyny

a circle of judgement
hangs around my life
chaining me to a sentence
worse than death

my worth
determined
by the prejudice of men
i've never even met

were i to instead aspire
to their expectations
and desires
in my own eyes, at least
i'd be worth less

no longer a person,
but an object to possess

the musings of dogs

look at that pussy
on the wall
do you think she'd come
if i call

maybe so,
maybe not
but now i've got
a better thought

i'll grab that little pussy
by the tail
won't it be funny
to hear her wail

- all my favorite men are dead -

it's not the names that break us

i'm drunk
i'm drunk
the 'bitch' said
to the 'slut'
before a man
raped them both
i guess it doesn't matter
what you're called
men will take advantage
no matter what

dreams of an untouchable me

i live in a world of hands

reaching   groping
stroking   hands
poking   prodding
judging   calling

     hands
   demanding
    i obey

touch you here
               then go over there
but no,
     not too far away

i'd try to hide
but hands can find
me
even in the darkest place

untouchable
is what i dream of
in the moments i devour
before a hand reaches out
to snatch
whatever makes me, me
away

for in a world of
wayward hands
only the untouchable
are safe

    - all my favorite men are dead -

- all my favorite men are dead -

i stayed silent
because i knew
i didn't have the strength
to carry what my truth would require
to withstand all of their ire
them, the bystanders
the faceless voices in the crowd
with no skin in the game –
metaphorically, literally –
yet only too happy to shame
any woman who dares
to stand up and claim
her all too real nightmares
in the light of day

i stayed silent
and every woman who knows
forgives me, i hope
and every woman who comes after
tries to do the same
as they are forced
to climb onto each other's shoulders
and shout what i could not even whisper

they are stronger
because they have no other choice
they must to survive
and all i can be
for the rest of their lives and mine
is so deeply, inexplicably sorry

help, she screams
to no one around
inside her head
so it doesn't make a sound

help someone
help me please
but no one can hear a girl
who's drowning
in her thoughts
who's dying
in her sleep

- all my favorite men are dead -

here but not here

i touch
but can't feel

look
but don't see

others think i'm crazy
but i know otherwise

i've grown numb
in my pain
to the world around
me

my life has become
defined
by the things i
don't want

the moments i
would unlive if i
could

everything i
would take back
toss out
undo i

exist in a negative space
consumed by
all that is missing
all that i
would replace

my fears –
not my joys –
are where i
spend my days
and the loneliness i
can't escape
comforts the life i
waste

- all my favorite men are dead -

remembering

i piled the debris
to one side
of my existence

this is where the garbage shall stay
i declared

and this is where i shall reside,
as i pointed to the other side

then proceeded to curl up
into the pile of life
mere moments ago
i'd so willingly
cast aside

i don't know myself

i don't know myself
i lost her
somewhere down a road
i never wanted to go

the thoughts in my head
are sometimes mine
sometimes not
and sometimes they're
not even thoughts

the beating of my heart
feels foreign in a chest
that was never meant to open
but must have at one point
because i can see through
every violent crack

every memory is clouded –
if they're even mine to claim –
they stay only as long as they like
and then, suddenly, go away

but there was a girl
i can still remember
once, long ago
who knew for certain
who she was
and in her body
felt at home

she seems now
but a fantasy
a fairytale told
to make life seem more tolerable
as the world grows cold

- all my favorite men are dead -

- all my favorite men are dead -

is no woman safe?

i watched my heroes fall
and knew their pain
i too, have been betrayed
i too, believed that good must win out
in the end
and i too, experienced the opposite
again and again
until finally – broken
i too, gave in

too far gone

your hand
pulls me back
from the entrance
of my grave

yet six feet under
i can barely hear
you calling my name

i'm sorry, but i think
this time
it's too late

- all my favorite men are dead -

for fear of speaking out

for fear of speaking out
for years i shut my mouth

internalized my pain
and so, immortalized their shame

i know no other way
for this life to play out

than cowered darkness
on display

the perpetuity of non-existence
set ablaze

desperate whispers in my head
unintelligible and vain

beseech me to give in
staking their claim

laid out underground
alone at last

the screams leave my body
a healing balm against an unchangeable past

like you did me

i put at once
this fire out
before it burnt us both

i smothered it
like you did me
until i could not but choke

- all my favorite men are dead -

- all my favorite men are dead -

depression

a curious darkness
swept over the sea

it danced and it played
with an unearthly symmetry

so entranced was i
by a world i could no longer see

i didn't realize until i lay asleep
that it had taken
everything from me

seven feet underground
i can finally hear the sound
of a heart beating in excitement
rather than fear

for once, in the nude
the scent of solitude
hangs lightly
in the air

beneath closed lids
i see what once was hid
on lips for which up was down
and down is now up

in the dark
there is a light
once lost in life
and the end
is blissfully here

- all my favorite men are dead -

i choose

the words came to me
one night
after i decided to stop trying
to take my own life
and they haven't stopped since
and i continue to write
and that's how i know
it won't be by my hand
i die
for every day, instead
i choose the pen
over the knife

a victim's prayer

give me more
oh goddess muse
i do adore
and pray to you
for words to scare
true monsters away –
the men who stalk my nights
and haunt my days

they lurk and linger
they smile and stare
and i must always be aware
lest fortune forsake me
in the arms of a 'friend'
and in an instant remember why
there are those
who wish for death

- *all my favorite men are dead* -

if i tell you
if i let you in
at this hour
to my darkest sins
what will it matter
if you liked me once
you won't anymore
i know it in my bones
in the depths of my dead soul
for who could love
such heinous thoughts?
who could withstand
all i cannot?

sane?

have you ever dreamt
of taking a hammer to your skull
just to watch all the broken pieces
shatter and fall

maybe not while i was asleep
but the thought has crossed my mind
several times
while lying awake at night
and another dozen or so more
while waiting in line
at the grocery store

- all my favorite men are dead -

i'm no longer in a dark place
i have become a dark place
and there's no escape

why i'm still alive

demons darken
the words i write
i care not
whether they offend or delight
i write to rid them of my mind
and in so doing,
achieve the peace i hope to find

- all my favorite men are dead -

tangled up inside myself

a mind of vines
strangling all reason and sense
has me
wishing
waiting
hoping
for death

just another before

which bad decision
shall be my last?

which moment
will decide the rest?

into which limb
shall the reaper's arrow soar?

on which day shall i become
just another soul who came before?

- all my favorite men are dead -

i lost my mind

i lost my mind
in a cloud
or did i lose my cloud
in a mind
was it ever even mine?
the cloud,
not the mind
or rather,
the intangible
fog i escape into
sometimes
when there's nowhere else
i can hide
to free myself
from this constant state
of dying
into which this plane
i've too long piloted
is flying

there are no gods
only demons
from a hell of our own making
they torture us
because they can
because we're all so needy

there are no miracles
only promises
we all continue breaking
until every heart's a mess
until every soul is bleeding

there is no joy
there is no love
only emotions we're all faking
for life is empty of all purpose
barren of all meaning

- all my favorite men are dead -

i come back to it
again and again
the wounds i lick
to remind me of when
my tongue was used
for kissing
for tasting
for talking
about more
than just
who i was before
you pinned me against the waves
just to watch them crash over my face
until all i could taste
was the salty sea spray
and blood from the bruises
you gave me
10 years ago
today

all my favorite men

all my favorite men are dead
and oft do i take
their corpses to bed

bodies that have long decayed
now pose no threat
to my desire to rest

and while
their hearts
and minds
and souls
remain

of and on this earth
they are – by rights
mine to take
to do with what i like
all that is left of their lives

and so, i take them
however i please
morning, noon, and night

some might cry
'but what of consent!'
to which i shall waste not my breath
nor hold my pen
happy in the knowledge
of my own intent

for unlike many alive today
and those long dead
whose unbled corpses
line my shelves
and fill the unclaimed spaces
in my head

the advantages i take
are not at the expense
of subjects objectified
beyond all reason and sense

but rather, objects
to which i can readily subject
my insatiable lust
for all that they have
and all that i must

the world may well be dimmer
had these 'great' men
never lived,
but in death
they finally pose my dear sisters
no immediate threat

and at least, like this
their past faults are easier to
forget
if not altogether forgive

- all my favorite men are dead -

a woman reborn

i buried myself today
broke new ground
to build my grave

for years
i carried a corpse
on my back

but today,
i wore black
and finally refused to fight back
a lifetime of tears

the body was weightless
had shrunk in my shame
yet still
took all my strength
to give her away

stone by stone
bone by bone
i let go
of the girl
i'd failed to protect

stepped back
into the world of men
a woman reborn
dangerous,
desirous only of
revenge

the war drum of my body

the language of my heart
is violence

it's both the music
and the dance

an organ of destruction
a soldier in my chest

each beat is an attack
another brush with death

the war drum of my body
forever crying out

kill all who cannot understand
kill all –
    even those we cannot live without

- all my favorite men are dead -

i don't want to be loved by men

i don't want to be loved by men
i want to confound them
perplex them
leave them
utterly depleted and defenseless
i want to consume their useless lives
the way they've consumed
the bodies and souls of women
for centuries

even now, swearing they'll be better
with their mouths full of our flesh
and a hunger in their eyes
even the blind can see
will never be quenched

so no,
i don't want to be loved by men
what i want
is to end them

finally

i can taste the fear on your lips
finally
it is i
who terrifies
finally
it is i
who shall sleep peacefully
tonight

- all my favorite men are dead -

i disarm men

not, as expected
with womanly charms

but through both the real
and imagined threat
of harm

i want them to understand

i don't want a fantasy
i want to frighten men
i want them to know
i want them to understand

- all my favorite men are dead -

- all my favorite men are dead -

there is a god
She is Me
I am She
and We
are here
to destroy
the patriarchy

the medusa'd men got only
what had always been coming to them
a woman's power knows no bounds
when hope is lost
and vengeance found

- all my favorite men are dead -

overdue abortion

cut a man open
only to watch him bleed
audacity and good fortune

i'd rather set fire to the bone
so i can watch him burn
an overdue abortion

but i can now

my words today
are the screams he silenced
and a child's trust he betrayed

she could not
but i can now

and every man should be afraid
for vengeance
is my vow

- all my favorite men are dead -

confession

'twas i
who set the house ablaze
with frightful unlit ice
a stony gaze
and womanly ways
destroyed
what all mankind believed
could never die
and the children
they had locked inside
were unwillingly
burnt alive

for whom do i give?

i'm trying to forgive
it's harder than it sounds
and i can't stop wondering
for whom do i give?
this gift
this kindness
until it is for me and me alone
i shall instead hold onto my hate
and make within it my home

- all my favorite men are dead -

- all my favorite men are dead -

and just think,

these poems i write
they spring from thoughts
that once ate me alive
i unleash them now
on the world of men
and hope that on them instead
they will wreak their havoc
and steal peace of mind
for mine has had all it can take
and just think,
'twas i the victim of their crimes
'twas my pain they so vehemently denied

assimilating

reflect what you see
to protect what you need
every day
wasted breaths spent
apologizing
for being
for seeing
for believing
both lies and truths
cannot be rebreathed
offer no reprieve
from the unsafety
you feel when 'free'
so i say again,
reflect what you see —
by whatever means —
to protect what you need
you owe this world nothing else
until it unconditionally respects
your humanity

- all my favorite men are dead -

I am a woman
girl in childhood
female since birth

yet i still don't know
what it means
to bear the weight of a womb
without considering myself
an object
for whom
my body will one day
be a home

no longer mine alone
was i – it?
created only to be shared?
with men
and then
all they care
to create, to propagate
to one day dominate

bring forth
into this world
a yet unknown clone
until half are decreed
people; free
and half are chained
to a half-reality

i hate this word –
woman –
banish the thought!

i exist.
what more needs to be said?

- all my favorite men are dead -

unattainable

no matter how high i climb
the bar is ever
just out of reach
even at the top
it seems
i must learn how to fly
if i would succeed

but women are not birds
and it's no secret that
Victoria's wings don't work
like they should
weighing us down
instead of lifting us
up into the clouds

perhaps if i jumped...
i start to think
maybe the tip of my finger
at least
could brush up against
all that i strive to be

can ideals be transferred
or is flesh too thick
for fantasy to penetrate –
i wonder and prepare to leap
from the somewhat more secure perch
i and my delusions
have worked so tirelessly
to reach

but at the last moment
i look down – finally un-dazzled
by all that lies
just above
my desire to gratify
and see a ground littered
with shattered dreams
the broken bodies of every
woman
who came before me

those poor deceived few
who desired to model
the roles
we're all expected to assume

i heed their unintended warning
and turn from my fate
hated for my choice
and the sacrifice
i refused to make

light me up
and i'll welcome the flames
like old friends

"i've known you before,"
i'd say

"and i'll know you again…
one day"

- all my favorite men are dead -

- all my favorite men are dead -

**for what is a witch, but a woman
hated by men**

witchcraft awakens
what the world
wouldn't witness

women
with the power
of creation deemed
an abomination

women
with the knowledge
to heal
burned alive

the truth
of men's hatred
revealed

our bodies remember

the world forgot
their names in time
but their pain –
it lingers

an inescapable burden
to which we all
are willfully resigned

- all my favorite men are dead -

- all my favorite men are dead -

line my coffin
with the bones
of the women
buried alive
before their time

mourn not
the loss of one
poor soul
but the death
of All
men could not bear
to live with

i know that girl
her pain is my own
but not mine alone
it's shared by all the women
who have suffered
and been struck down
by the stones
sinful men throw

- all my favorite men are dead -

remember me mad
remember me angry
remember me a wild fire
burning everything you love to the ground
remember me a thousand feet down
beneath your feet
food for the worms
and yet still refusing to admit defeat
remember me untamable
unbroken, unshakeable
remember me with chills
sprinting up your spine
remember me shrill
a woman's voice to the end
a woman's walk
a woman's body
a woman's mind
a woman's way of living
and when it's up –
a woman's time
remember me
unapologetic through it all
remember me
remember me
remember me
else throw all memory of me to the wolves
on the wind, lost to the waves
even gone still brave, still hungry, still untamed
and coward that you are
unable to forget, unwilling to remember
be done with my name
for it was always *mine alone* to claim

i will never not have been raped

if healing
means living
as if my life had never happened
i don't really see
how it's possible to heal
and still be Me

2am, and the chill in the air –
indifferent to my wishes
unconcerned with my resistance –
molests my exposed flesh

the strains of the bass thumping
and men humping
women whose hearts are unconscious
stalk me out of a bar
i never should have entered

desperate to erase the pain
i drag my hands along the walls
that lead the way
ripping them open
from knuckle to wrist

begging into the void
    for the music
    and the memories
    the sounds
    the screams
    the ear-splitting soundless pleas
to stop

but a traitorous inner voice persists
whispering fear into my heart
cruelly insisting

it will never get better

they will never get better

- all my favorite men are dead -

this world will never get better

nothing will ever get better

the realization is a burglar
breaking and entering my body
taking all the hope i had left
and leaving me, empty
with nothing but a scrap of unwanted truth:

this life,
this body,
are a purgatory from which
no amount of prayer will
ever
enable me to escape

.

.

.

a bloody trail
leads to the middle of an unlit bridge

and the girl
who couldn't stop wondering

what are you supposed to do,
when you no longer want to live
but are too afraid to die?

is gone.

- all my favorite men are dead -

it's true
the girl is gone...
but her heart lives on
in the woman i've found
the woman i've become

- all my favorite men are dead -

when the dust settles

all the good intentions in the world
can't change what has been done
and justice – that poor old chap
can't fight a war that's won

it happened to me too
that thing you don't speak about
and even though i don't speak about it either
i just wanted you to know
you're not alone
i see the pain you never show
i've heard the screams that burn inside your throat
i taste the tears you cry at night
so even you can't see
how much this world has broken you
and though it can't possibly lighten your load
or take away the pain
i hope it helps
in some small way
to know this world has also broken me

and yet, somehow
still
i continue to be

Acknowledgments

There are a million thanks I need to give – not just for the creation of this book, but for the fact that I'm alive to write it at all. There are so many people I need to thank in my life for bringing me to this moment, some of whom I've never even known their names. Kind strangers who gave me enough hope to get me through some dark days, particularly the woman driving down a dark bridge in Bali on the night of the blood wolf moon whose kindness saved a life. But also, very dear friends – Monica, Bria, Natalie, Araceli, Clay, Jacob, Claudia – who have been there for me in so many ways and made life feel full when I was running on empty. My family – Momma Cindy, Chaddy, Aunt Jill, Cameron, Sandor, Jenny, Frances – who remind me that family are the people who you choose and who choose you.

I also want to thank my editor, Shelby Leigh, and my graphic designer, Chris Reale for believing in this book and giving me the encouragement and confidence to see it through.

Then there's the lesser thanks (though no less important) to all of the women who have transformed their pain into beautiful art that made me feel less alone throughout my life: Louisa May Alcott, Jane Austen, Margaret Atwood, Kerry Cohen, Bernardine Evaristo, Naomi Alderman, Taylor Swift, Olivia Rodrigo, Halsey, Pink, Billie Eilish, Aretha Franklin, Dolly Parton, The Dixie Chicks, Marren Morris, Martina McBride, Sylvia Plath, Emily Dickinson, Rupi Kaur, Henley Worthen, Ari B. Cofer, Kate Baer, Alexandra Vasiliu, and countless more I'm sure I'm forgetting in this moment, but whose words were a healing balm in hard times.

Thank you to every single person who has gone out of their way to love me, support me, see me, validate me, care for me and – in so doing – help me live through what I didn't think I could.

Why are these things always written in 3rd person?
Hey babes, I'm Kate (aka női lélek). I'm an american of Hungarian-Italian descent currently living in Los Angeles. I've traveled to over 56 countries, I ride a motorcycle, and I write poetry to keep myself alive - literally. I wrote my first poem the night after  I tried to commit suicide for the last time and I've never looked back. If you have any questions for me, want to say hi, or even if you're just feeling lonely in this world, reach out to me on my insta @noilelek or on my website noilelek.com. I'd love to hear from you and help in any way I can!